Mei-yin May Lewis

Easy Hong Kong Cooking at Home

Outskirts Press, Inc.
Denver, Colorado

Easy Hong Kong Cooking at Home
All Rights Reserved.
Copyright © 2008 Mei-yin May Lewis
v 3.0

Outskirts Press, Inc.
http://www.outskirtspress.com

ISBN: 978-1-4327-1971-5

Library of Congress Number: 2008921501

Outskirts Press and the "OP" logo are trademarks belonging to Outskirts Press, Inc.

PRINTED IN THE UNITED STATES OF AMERICA

Preface

Although Hong Kong inherits her cuisine from Guangzhou, China; the meeting of the eastern and western cultures has led to much improvement in the preparation and serving of the traditional dishes. It is why the city of Hong Kong has achieved the title "ideal eating out in Hong Kong." As a result of its distinctive commercial and historical influences, Hong Kong is not only well known for its Southern Chinese cooking, but also famous for its "East meets West" international fare. Combining local Hong Kong with other countries' cooking methods and ingredients creates "Fusion" Hong Kong dishes. I was lucky to be raised in Hong Kong and have enjoyed a great variety of cuisines.

I remember when I was studied abroad, I did not have a car, and so walking a long distance to the nearest Chinese restaurant or take-out shop were the only way to satisfy my Chinese food craving. However, I was always disappointed because the food was never as delicious as I had expected. After I graduated and moved back to Hong Kong, I made sure not miss any opportunities to eat out. The variety of options was vast, since there are so many different Chinese Provinces' cuisines, as well as Vietnamese, Thai, American, Spanish, Indian and Japanese restaurants. I became interested in cooking and realized that cooking Hong Kong Chinese cuisine is not just fun but also very creative. Since then, cooking for others has always been a personal pleasure in my life. Not surprisingly, my interest in cooking has developed into a teaching career. As a cooking instructor, I enjoy sharing my knowledge and experience in cooking with people who love Hong Kong Cuisine.

My family moves around a lot due to my husband's job and many of the places we've called home did not have Chinatowns. The local small Chinese restaurants, often adjusted to American palates and thus inauthentic, were our only options when we wanted to eat Chinese food. Knowing how to cook Hong Kong Chinese cuisine is not only a money-saving alternative to dining, but it also satisfies my desire of having a high-quality and healthy meals with my loved ones.

Personally, I enjoy tasting and trying out different cuisines, from Chinese to western, and from authentic to contemporary. When I try different Chinese cuisines, I am inspired to create new combinations and experiment with new ways of cooking. Using simple ingredients that one can be obtained locally, I highly recommend these 45 recipes to people that wish to enjoy their own deliciously easy Hong Kong dishes at home. Of these recipes, some are traditional incorporated with new ideas; and some are newly created from traditional ingredients. Each recipe comes with detailed cooking instruction and a list of ingredients that are commonly available at your local grocery stores or Asian markets. The method of cooking is easy to follow and prepare at home. Even beginners and those who are discouraged by the lack of authentic Chinese ingredients will find these recipes appealing. I hope you will enjoy making these creative recipes with those you love. Recipes made with love and care are sure to be tasty!

Dedication

To my husband, Ernest,
My lovely child, Kam,
My family,
My Brother-in-law, George,
My friends, Andrea, Jessica and Katy,
Thank you for inspiring and helping me through
so many ways in my cooking and teaching career.

Content

Seafood

Vegetables and Tofu

Rice and Noodle

Essential Ingredients in Hong Kong Home Cooking

Deep-fried Chicken Wings with Fermented Bean Curd

(4 servings)

Ingredients:

Chicken wings	12 pieces
Oil	1 cup
Sliced cucumber	1 whole (for garnish)

Marinade:

Fermented bean curd	2 tbsp
Salt	½ tsp
Five spice powder	½ tsp
Dried galangal powder	½ tsp
Shao Hsing wine	½ tbsp
Beaten egg	1

Method:

1. Wash and wipe dry the chicken wings; marinate with fermented bean curd, salt, five spice powder, galangal powder, Shao Hsing wine, and beaten egg for 1 hour.
2. Heat wok on high heat for 20 seconds, then add 1 cup of oil into it, lower the chicken wings into the wok, and deep-fry over high heat until they are fully cooked.
3. Garnish cucumber on the plate and arrange chicken wings in the middle of the plate.

Tips:
Do not keep turning the chicken wings after lowering them into the wok; otherwise the fermented bean curd batter may come off. Cook one side of the wings at a time; then turn to cook other side after one side is done.

Lychee Chicken

(4 servings)

Ingredients:

Chicken breasts	3 pieces (skinless and boneless)
Green bell pepper	1 whole
Onion	1 half
Red bell pepper	1 whole
Canned lychee	12 pieces
Oil	1 cups
All-purpose flour	3 tbsp

Seasoning:

Soy sauce	½ tbsp
Salt	½ tsp
White pepper	⅛ tsp
Water	1 tbsp
Custard powder	1 tbsp

Sauce:

Ketchup	4 tbsp
White vinegar	1 tbsp
Sugar	2 tbsp
Worcestershire sauce	1 tsp
Salt	¼ tsp
Water	¼ cup

Method:

1. Cut chicken breasts into 2-3 inch pieces. Season chicken with soy sauce, salt, white pepper, water, and custard powder for 15 minutes.
2. Cut and clean green bell pepper, red bell pepper, and onion into pieces, similar to the chicken pieces' size. Mix sauce ingredients in a small bowl for later use.
3. Coat chicken meat with all-purpose flour. Heat a non-stick skillet on high heat for 20 seconds, and then add oil into the skillet. Then turn the heat down to medium high immediately. Put the chicken into the skillet and fry until golden brown. Drain oil on paper towel.
4. Leave 1 tbsp of oil in the wok over medium high heat, sauté green bell pepper, red bell pepper, and onion for 2 minutes. Add the mixed sauce into the wok and brings to boil.
5. Lastly, stir in lychee and chicken, mix well. Dish on a serving plate.

Tips:

One tbsp of custard powder can be substituted by 1 egg. In Hong Kong, custard powder is widely used in local restaurants since they add more color to food and do not burn as easily as eggs. Custard powder can be found in larger grocery stores and British grocery stores.

Minced Chicken Patties with Sesame Seed

(4 servings)

Ingredients:

Minced chicken	1 pound
Chinese parsley	4 stalks
Onion powder	½ tsp
Garlic powder	½ tsp
Five spice powder	½ tsp
Sugar	½ tsp
Soy sauce	1 tbsp
Salt	¼ tsp
Tapioca flour	1 tbsp
Black sesame seeds	½ cup
White sesame seeds	½ cup
Oil	4 tbsp
Chinese parsley	garnish

Method:

1. Finely chop Chinese parsley. Add Chinese parsley, onion powder, garlic powder, five spice powder, sugar, soy sauce, salt, and tapioca flour into the minced chicken and mix well.
2. Put white sesame seeds on one plate and black sesame seeds on another plate.
3. Shape the minced chicken into 12 individual round-shaped meat patties.
4. Dip one side of each of the chicken patties into the white sesame seeds and then dip the other side into the black sesame seeds.
5. Heat 4 tbsp of oil in a non-stick pan, and pan-fry the chicken patties over medium heat for 5 - 7 minutes on each side until they are done.
6. Place patties on serving plate and garnish with Chinese parsley.

Tips:

Using medium heat can avoid the burning of the white sesame seeds, since sesame seeds cook quickly. Controlling the heat is very important.

Three Cups Chicken

(4 servings)

Ingredients:

Chicken thighs	8 pieces
Sesame oil	½ cup
Spring onion	3 stalks
Garlic	3 cloves
Ginger	6 slices
Carrot	12 slices
Water	2 cups

Seasoning:

Dark soy sauce	5 tbsp
Soy sauce	2 tbsp
Shao Hsing wine	½ cup
Sugar	2 tsp

Method:

1. Clean and pat dry chicken thighs, then cut each thigh in half. Cut garlic in half. Cut spring onions into 3 inches long pieces. Shape carrot slices into flowers by using cookies cutters.
2. Boil 2 cups of water in a pot; then add 3 slices of ginger and 1 stalk of spring onion into water. Boil chicken pieces for 2 minutes. Drain and discard water.
3. Heat ½ cup of sesame oil in a clay pot over high heat. Sauté garlic, ginger, and spring onions for 20 seconds. Add the chicken into the clay pot, sauté for an additional 2 minutes. Add dark soy sauce, soy sauce, sugar and wine into the pot, turn the heat to medium and cook for 25 minutes. Cover with lid. Turn the chicken 2-3 times while cooking to make sure they are all colored evenly.
4. Add the carrot flowers into the clay pot and cook for another 2 minutes.
5. Serve hot.

Tips:
Whole chicken or chicken wings can be used if chicken thighs are not available. Wok can be used instead of clay pot.

Shredded Chicken with
Five Spice Oyster Flavored Sauce

(4 servings)

Ingredients:

Whole chicken	1 piece
Spring onion	4 stalks
Bay leaf	1 piece
Aniseeds	2 pieces
Five spice powder	1 tsp
Oyster flavored Sauce	2 tbsp
Salt	½ tsp
Sugar	½ tsp
Chicken stock	4 cups
Water	2 cups
Oil	3 tbsp

Method:

1. Add the canned chicken stock, water, bay leaf, and aniseeds into a large pot. Bring soup to boil at high heat, lower the chicken into soup. Turn to low heat, and simmer for 20 minutes. Then turn off the heat, but do not open the lid and keep the chicken into the soup for another 20 minutes.
2. Mix the five spice powder, oyster favored sauce, salt, and sugar together for the sauce. Reserve for later use.
3. Finely chop the spring onion. Use a small pan, heat oil over high heat for about 1 minute and pour the hot oil over the spring onion.
4. Take the chicken out, let it cool down a bit. Shred the chicken meat into long thin strips by hand. Pour the five spice sauce mix on top. Then spoon 2 - 3 spoonfuls of spring onion on top.

Tips:

Whole chicken is about 2 pound and can also be substituted by 6 pieces of chicken legs.

Honey Sesame Chicken

(4 servings)

Ingredients:

Skinless, boneless chicken beast	2 pieces
Canned button mushrooms	1 can
Sesame seeds	1 tbsp
Oil	1 cup

Marinade:

Soy sauce	1 tsp
Salt	½ tsp
Sugar	½ tsp
Ginger wine	1 tsp
Sesame oil	½ tsp
Water	1 tbsp
Tapioca flour	2 tbsp

Sauce:

Honey	2 tbsp
Ketchup	1 tbsp
Soy sauce	1 tbsp
Water	2 tbsp

Method:
1. Clean and pat dry the chicken breast meat, cut into 2 inches pieces, then marinate with soy sauce, salt, sugar, ginger wine, sesame oil, and water for 30 minutes. Drain button mushrooms and set aside.
2. Heat a pan on medium high heat; put 1 tbsp of white sesame seeds in the pan, and dry toast for 20-30 seconds. Keep tossing with a Chinese spatula until sesame seeds turn light brown. Remove from pan immediately.
3. Coat chicken with tapioca flour. Heat 1 cup of oil on high heat in a wok; fry chicken pieces until they are done. Discard the oil. Remove and drain the chicken pieces.
4. Heat 1 tbsp of oil in a pan, sauté sliced button mushroom for 1 minute. Stir in honey, ketchup, soy sauce, and water in a pan and bring to a boil. Add chicken into the sauce and toss well. Sprinkle toasted white sesame seeds on top.

Tips:
Do not over toast sesame seeds as they will keep cooking even after being removed from a hot pan.

Stir-fried Chicken with Thai Style Sweet Chili Sauce

(4 servings)

Ingredients:

Chicken meat	2 pieces (boneless and skinless)
Chinese broccoli	4 oz
Carrot flowers	6 slices
Minced garlic	2 tbsp
Spring onion	3 stalks
Basil leaves	2 – 3 stalks
Thai sweet chili sauce	3 tbsp
Chicken stock	1 cup
Oil	3 tbsp
Shao Hsing wine	1 tsp

Seasoning:

Fish sauce	2 tbsp
Salt	¼ tsp
Lime juice	½ tbsp
Water	1 tbsp
Cornstarch	¼ tsp

Method:

1. Wash and pat dry chicken meat and cut into long thin strips.
2. Wash and dry Chinese broccoli, then cut into about 3 inch long pieces. Cut spring onion into about 3 inch long pieces as well.
3. Boil chicken stock with 1 tbsp of oil, and blanch Chinese broccoli for 2 minutes. Remove from boiling stock and set aside. Shape carrot slices into flower shape by using a flower shape cookie cutter.
4. Heat a wok over high heat for 30 seconds and use 2 tbsp of oil to sauté garlic and spring onion for 10 seconds,. Then add chicken meat into the wok, and sprinkle wine over chicken. Quickly stir-fry for about 5 minutes, until the chicken is almost done.
5. Add blanched Chinese broccoli, basil, and carrot flowers into the wok and mix well with a Chinese spatula. Add sweet chili sauce, fish sauce, salt, lime juice, water, and cornstarch into the wok and stir-fry with chicken meat until the sauce boils again and becomes thickened.

Tips:

Asparagus can substitute Chinese broccoli. Thai sweet chili sauce is sold in Asian markets and big supermarkets.

Coconut Curry Chicken

(4 servings)

Ingredients:

Boneless skinless chicken breast	2 pieces
Onion	1 small
Green bell pepper	1 small
Potato	1 medium
Minced garlic	1 tsp
Bay leaves	3 pieces
Garam Masala	1 tsp
Curry powder	1 tsp
Coconut milk	⅔ cup
Salt	½ tsp
Sugar	1 tsp
Water	1 cup
Oil	2 cups

Seasoning:

Salt	½ tsp
Soy sauce	1 tsp
White pepper	¼ tsp
Cornstarch	1 tbsp

Method:

1. Clean and cut the chicken into 1 inch pieces. Season the chicken with salt, soy sauce, white pepper, and cornstarch for 30 minutes.
2. Cut potato, onion, and green bell pepper into about 1 inch pieces as well.
3. Heat 2 cups of oil on high heat in a wok, deep fry potato pieces until brown. Remove potato pieces from oil. Use the same oil to blanch chicken meat on high heat for 1 minute. Then remove the chicken and discard the oil.
4. Put 2 tbsp of oil in a clean wok, use medium high heat to sauté minced garlic for 10 seconds, add onion into the wok and sauté for 2 minutes; and then add green bell pepper into the wok, and sauté with onion for 1 minute.
5. Add bay leaves, curry powder and Garam Masala powder into the wok, stir well with vegetables. Place the chicken cubes and potato into the wok. At the same time, add water into the wok. Cover with a wok lid and bring to boil for 5 minutes.
6. Remove the wok lid and add coconut milk, sugar, and salt, cover and simmer over medium low heat for 5 minutes until potato pieces are tender.

Tips:

Add salt can accentuate the coconut taste.

Garam Masala is a mixed spice powder which can be found in Asian and Indian grocery shops. It can enhance the curry aroma and flavor.

Soy Sauce Chicken Wings

(4 servings)

Ingredients:

Chicken wings	8 pieces
Spring onion	4 stalks
Ginger	4 slices
Dark soy sauce	1/3 cup
Soy sauce	2/3 cup
Water	1 cup
Star anise	3 pieces
Sichuan peppercorns	1 tbsp
Rock sugar	1 – 1 ¼ cup (to taste)

Method:
1. Wash and pat dry the chicken wings and cut them into half. Cut spring onion into 3 inch pieces.
2. Add spring onion, ginger slices and about 3 cups of water in a wok (water level should be able to cover the chicken wings; if not, then add more water), and bring to a boil. Place the chicken wings in the wok and cover with a wok lid, boil the wings for 2 minutes. Turn off the heat and transfer the chicken wings to cold tap water for a few minutes.
3. Add dark soy sauce, soy sauce, water, star anise, Sichuan peppercorns, and rock sugar in a clean wok and bring to boil over high heat. Taste to see whether the soy sauce is sweet enough; if it is not, add more rock sugar into it.
4. After adjusting the soy sauce to the flavor of your tastes, lower the chicken wings into the soy sauce and cover with a wok lid. Boil for a minute and then turn off the heat, let the chicken wings sit in the wok for 20 minutes.

5. After 20 minutes, remove chicken wings from soy sauce and arrange on the serving plate.

Tips:
The soy sauce can be used again and be stored in the refrigerator for up to a week.

Western Style Short Ribs

(4 servings)

Ingredients:

Beef short ribs	1 pound
Red onion	1 medium
Red bell pepper	1 small
Minced garlic	1 tsp
Oil	½ cup

Marinade:

Soy sauce	2 tsp
Baking soda	⅛ tsp
Sugar	1 tsp
Cornstarch	1 tsp
Water	3 tbsp
Shao Hsing wine	2 tsp

Sauce:

Salt	½ tsp
Sugar	1 tsp
Tapioca flour	1 tsp
Ketchup,	2 tbsp
Steak sauce	2 tbsp
Worcestershire sauce	1 tbsp
Water	4 tbsp

Method:
1. Clean and cut the beef short ribs into small sections. Marinate beef short ribs with soy sauce, baking soda, sugar, cornstarch, water and wine for 30 minutes.
2. Cut red onion and red bell pepper into big pieces.
3. Combine all sauce ingredients in a small bowl.
4. Put ½ cup of oil in a wok on medium high heat and pan-fry the short ribs until medium well. Remove from wok.
5. Leave 1 tbsp of oil in the wok, use high heat to sauté minced garlic, red onion, and red bell pepper for about 2 - 3 minutes. Put the short ribs back into the wok and pour sauce over it. Cook until the sauce has thickened. Dish up on a serving plate.

Tips:
Onion and celery can be used instead of red onion and red bell pepper.

Roasted Pork Belly

(4 servings)

Ingredients:

Pork belly	2 pounds
Salt	1 ½ cups
Shredded spring onion	1 stalk
Honey mustard	2 tbsp

Marinade:

Sugar	1 tsp
Salt	1 tsp
Chinese rose-wine or gin	1 tbsp
Five-spice powder	1 tsp

Method:

1. Rinse pork belly and wipe dry with paper towel. Poke the skin with the tip of a knife evenly. Rub sugar, salt, Chinese rose wine and five-spice powder on the pork belly evenly and marinate it for 2 hours. Wipe dry with paper towel before baking in the oven.
2. Preheat oven to 400°F. Place a foil paper on a baking tray.
3. Arrange pork belly in a baking tray with the skin side up. Cover the pork belly completely in salt. Bake at 400°F for 45 minutes until it is done. Remove from heat. Scrape away the salt with a knife. Discard the used foil paper and replace a new foil paper on the baking tray. Place the pork belly on the clean foil paper tray again. Switch the oven to broil and bake again at 450°F for 30-45 minutes until the skin turns golden and crunchy.
4. Remove from heat and leave it to cool. Chop into pieces. Garnish with shredded spring onion and honey mustard. Serve.

Tips:

Poke more holes on the pork belly skin with a knife will increase the crunchiness.

Beef with Oyster Flavored Sauce

(4 servings)

Ingredients:

Beef steak	8 oz
Choy Sum	8 oz
Spring onion	1 stalk
Ginger	3 slices
Chicken stock	1 cup
Minced garlic	2 cloves
Water	1 cup
Oil	2 ½ tbsp

Marinade:

Baking soda	¼ tsp
Water	3 tbsp
Sugar	1 tsp
Soy sauce	1 tbsp
Cornstarch	1 tsp

Sauce:

Oyster flavored sauce	2 tbsp
Sugar	1 tsp
Soy sauce	1 tsp
Dark soy sauce	1 tsp
Cornstarch	½ tsp
Sesame oil	½ tsp
Water	½ cup

Method:
1. Slice beef steak into 2 mm-thick slices and marinate with baking soda, water, sugar, soy sauce, and cornstarch for 30 minutes. In a different bowl, mix all the sauce ingredients for later use.
2. Wash choy sum thoroughly, cut spring onion into 3 inch long pieces.
3. Combine 1 cup of water and 1 cup of chicken stock, half tbsp of oil and ginger slices in a wok. Bring to a boil, add choy sum into the wok and boil for 3 - 5 minutes until tender. Drain water and arrange choy sum on a serving plate.
4. Heat 2 tbsp of oil over high in a wok, sauté minced garlic and spring onion, then add sliced beef and stir-fry until beef is almost done. Discard the spring onion. Add the sauce mixture into the wok, and cook until the sauce is thickened, then pour over choy sum in a serving plate. Serve hot.

Tips:
Other vegetables, such as green bell pepper, broccoli, or lettuce can be used instead of choy sum.

Stir-fried Pork Cubes with Cashew Nuts in Crispy Wrap

(4 servings)

Ingredients:

Lean pork meat	6 oz
Red bell pepper	1 half
Zucchini	1 whole
Carrot	1 whole
Ginger	3 slices
Minced shallot	1 tbsp
Minced garlic	1 tbsp
Raw cashew nuts	½ cup
Spring roll sheet	1 piece
Oil	1 cup
Shao Hsing wine	1 tsp
Shredded lettuce	garnish
Shredded carrot	garnish

Seasoning:

Salt	¼ tsp
Soy sauce	1 tsp
Sugar	½ tsp
Tapioca flour	½ tsp
Water	2 tbsp
Oil	1 tsp

Sauce:

Water	3 tbsp
Salt	¼ tsp
Chicken powder	¼ tsp
Tapioca flour	½ tsp
Sesame oil	½ tsp

Method:

1. Boil 2 cups of water in a wok; add cashew nuts and boil for 2 minutes. Drain nuts and dry in a strainer. Heat 1 cup of oil over medium heat in a wok, deep-fry cashew nuts until color turns golden brown.
2. Wash and wipe dry the pork meat; cut into 1 cm-sized cubes. Season the pork cubes with salt, soy sauce, sugar, tapioca flour, water, and oil for 30 minutes.
3. Prepare the sauce in a bowl for later use.
4. Dice the red bell pepper, zucchini, and carrot into 1 – 2 cm pieces.
5. Place the spring roll sheet in a round oven safe bowl. Preheat the oven on 400°F, and bake the spring roll sheet for 3 minutes or until golden brown. Place on a serving plate and garnish with shredded lettuce and shredded carrot around the spring roll sheet.
6. Heat 1 tbsp of oil over high heat in a wok, sauté the diced red bell pepper, diced zucchini and diced carrot, stirring constantly with a Chinese spatula for 2 minutes. Remove from wok and set aside.

7. Heat 2 tbsp of oil over high heat in a wok; then stir-fry the minced garlic, shallot, and pork cubes until the meat is done.
8. Add vegetables into the wok, sauté for a minute. Sprinkle Shao Hsing wine on top and mix well; toss the deep-fried cashew nuts into it; and then add the sauce mixture into the wok and stir until the sauce is thickened. Dish up into the baked spring roll sheet.

Tips:
Place the cooked meat and vegetables inside the spring roll sheet right before ready to eat because the spring roll sheet becomes soggy once it touches the hot cooked food.

Braised ChinKiang Vinegar Pork Ribs

(4 servings)

Ingredients:

Spare ribs	1 ½ pound
Sliced shallot	2 pieces
Ginger	3 slices
Spring onion	2 stalks
ChinKiang vinegar	1/3 cup
Soy sauce	1 tbsp
Dark soy sauce	1 tbsp
Rock sugar	100 g (about 2 - 3 big pieces)
Water	⅓ cup
Oil	2 tbsp
Spring onion	a few (for garnish)

Method:

1. Wash and wipe dry spare ribs. Cut spring onion into 3 inch pieces.
2. Heat the wok on high heat for 30 seconds; then add 2 tbsp of oil into the wok to sauté shallot, ginger, and spring onion for a minute. Add the spare ribs into the wok and brown both side.
3. Add Chinkiang vinegar, soy sauce, dark soy sauce, rock sugar, and water into the wok and bring to boil. Once boiling, turn the heat to medium low heat and braise for 30-45 minutes until the meat is tender and the sauce is thickened. Place on dish. Garnish with spring onion.

Tips:
ChinKiang vinegar and rock sugar are sold in Asian markets, and rock sugar can be substituted by light brown sugar.

Stir-fried Pork Ribs with Leek

(4 servings)

Ingredients:

Spare ribs	8 oz
Leek	2 stalks
Water	2 cups and 3 tbsp
Oil	2 tbsp
Minced garlic	1 tsp
Minced shallot	1 tsp
Shao Hsing wine	½ tsp
Chu Hou sauce	1 tsp
Hoi Sin Sauce	1 tsp
Dark soy sauce	½ tsp
Sugar	½ tsp

Marinade:

Salt	½ tsp
Soy sauce	1 tsp
Chicken powder	½ tsp
Water	2 tbsp
Tapioca flour	½ tsp

Method:

1. Wash and wipe dry spare ribs and cut into 1 - 2 inch pieces. Marinate spare ribs with salt, soy sauce, chicken powder, water, and tapioca flour for 30 minutes
2. Wash and cut the white parts of the leek diagonally. Discard the green parts.
3. Boil 2 cups of water in a wok, and blanch leeks for 1 minute. Drain leeks in a colander.
4. Heat 2 tbsp of oil over high heat in a wok. Add minced garlic and minced shallots into the oil and sauté for 20 seconds.
5. Add pork ribs into the wok and sauté ribs, stirring with Chinese spatula constantly for 3 minutes. Sprinkle wine over the pork, and then add chu hou sauce, hoi sin sauce, dark soy sauce, 3 tbsp of water, and sugar into the wok immediately. Stir-fry until all the sauce is mixed well with the pork, then cover with wok lid and cook over medium heat for 20 minutes.
6. Add the blanched leek into the wok, and sauté with pork for 1 minute.
7. Dish up and serve hot.

Tips:

To enhance leek's flavor, leave leek in a cool and dry place for 2 -3 days until it is a bit dried out and turns yellowish in color.

Sautéed Beef with Black Pepper Sauce on Hot Grill Pan

(4 servings)

Ingredients:

Beef steak	8 oz
Onion	½ piece
Green bell pepper	½ piece
Red bell pepper	½ piece
Crushed black pepper	1 tsp
Shao Hsing wine	1 tsp
Minced garlic	1 clove
Oil	2 tbsp

Marinade:

Water	5 tbsp
Oyster flavored sauce	1 tbsp
Soy sauce	½ tsp
Sugar	½ tsp
Baking soda	¼ tsp
Cornstarch	1 tsp

Sauce:

Soy sauce	1 tbsp
Sugar	½ tsp
Black pepper	½ tsp
Sesame oil	a few drops
Water	3 tbsp
Cornstarch	1 tsp

Method:

1. Slice beef into 2 inches thin long strips. Mix all the marinade ingredients in a bowl. Add beef strips into it and marinate for 30 minutes.
2. Wash and clean onion, green bell pepper, and red bell pepper. Cut all the vegetables into 2 inches thin long strips like the beef
3. Prepare the sauce in a measuring cup for later use.
4. Heat 1 tbsp of oil in a non-stick fry pan for 30 seconds, and sauté beef strips to medium well. Remove from wok and set aside.
5. Preheat the oven at 400°F, and then put the grill pan into preheated oven for 5 minutes.
6. Meanwhile, heat 1 tbsp of oil in a pan for 30 seconds, add crushed black pepper and minced garlic in the pan, sauté for one minute until fragrant. Add onion, green bell pepper and red bell pepper into the pan, stir fry until all the vegetables are done, then add beef strips, wine and sauce in the pan. Stir-fry until the sauce is bought to a boil.
7. Move the hot grill pan from oven onto the wooden mat. Transfer the food to the hot grill pan carefully. Serve hot.

Tips:
Caution: The hot grill pan is very hot and has to be handled with care.

Steamed Minced Pork Tic-Tac-Toe

(4 servings)

Ingredients:

Minced pork	1 pound
Chinese mushrooms	2 -3 pieces
Fresh water chestnuts	8 pieces
Carrot	4 -5 thin slices
Water	3 cups

Marinade:

Salt	¼ tsp
Sugar	½ tsp
Soy sauce	1 tbsp
Sesame oil	1 tsp
Water	2 tbsp
Shao Hsing wine	1 tsp
Cornstarch	1 tsp

Method:

1. Soak the Chinese mushrooms in water for 1 hour, and cut the stems off when it is softened. Rub cornstarch on the Chinese mushrooms and then rinse well.
2. Mix salt, sugar, soy sauce, sesame oil, wine, water, and cornstarch in a bowl. Add minced pork into the bowl and mix well, marinate for 30 minutes.
3. Meanwhile, slice one Chinese mushroom into 2 mm thin slices and trim them to about 1 inch long thin strips. Put two strips in a group. And then mince another one.
4. Wash and peel the skin off the water chestnuts. And then mince water chestnuts. Divide into two portions.
5. Mix minced mushrooms and one portion of water chestnut with the minced pork, spread on a deep plate and shape it into a square. Arrange another half of minced water chestnuts on top of the minced pork into nine squares, like a Tic-Tac-Toe frame.
6. Place two strips of mushrooms like a cross on one square and put one slice of round carrot on another square, like playing Tic-Tac-Toe.
7. Add three cups of water to a wok; place a steam rack in the wok, cover with wok lid and brings to a boil. Put the plated dish into the wok and cover with lid, steam for 15 minutes. Serve hot.

Tips:

Canned water chestnuts can be used instead of fresh water chestnuts.
The leftover sauce from a dish is very delicious and good to serve over rice. Ask a young child to cook with you and play an edible Tic-Tac-Toe. It's fun!

Pan-fried Lotus Root Sandwiches

(4 servings)

Ingredients:

Lotus root	2 sections
Minced pork	4 oz
Finely chopped spring onion	1 stalk
Cornstarch	3 tbsp
Oil	3 tbsp
Soy sauce	2 tsp (if desired for dipping)

Seasoning:

Soy sauce	½ tbsp
Salt	½ tsp
Sugar	½ tsp
Sesame oil	½ tsp
White pepper	⅛ tsp
Cornstarch	1 tbsp
Water	1 tbsp

Method:

1. Wash lotus root sections, pat dry, and cut off the ends. Slice the lotus root into thin slices, about 2 - 3 mm thick. Prepare 2 slices as a group. Sprinkle some cornstarch on each side of lotus root pieces.
2. Mix all seasonings in a small bowl. Add the spring onion and minced pork and mix well.
3. Put 1 tbsp minced pork mixture on one slice of lotus root, and then add another slice on top, just like making sandwich.
4. Coat the lotus root sandwiches with cornstarch.
5. Heat a pan on high heat for 30 seconds; add 3 tbsp of oil into the pan. Lower the sandwiches into the pan and pan-fry sandwiches until they turn golden brown. Serve hot with soy sauce as desired.

Tips:

Cornstarch acts like a glue to attach minced pork in between two slices of lotus roots.

Golden Shrimp Purses

(4 servings)

Ingredients:

Large shrimps	12 pieces
Minced pork	½ cup
Minced water chestnuts	2 tbsp
Round dumpling wraps	12 pieces
Beaten egg	1
Oil	3 cups
Salt	¼ tsp
Tapioca starch	½ tbsp
Sliced lettuce	garnish

Seasoning:

Salt, Sugar, Soy sauce	¼ tsp each
White pepper	⅛ tsp
Cornstarch	½ tsp

Dipping Sauce:

Ketchup	3 tbsp
Worcestershire sauce	1 tsp
Tabasco, Soy sauce	½ tsp each

Method:

1. Clean, peel and de-vein the shrimps, leaving the tails on. Rub shrimps with salt and tapioca starch for a minute, and then rinse well with tap water. Dry with paper towel and set aside.
2. Combine all the seasoning with minced pork and mix well. Then add minced water chestnuts into the minced pork, and mix well again.
3. Place 1 teaspoonful of pork mixture in the center of a dumpling wrap, while keeping the remaining wraps covered with a damp cloth to prevent drying. Place one shrimp, tail side up, on top of the pork mixture. Brush beaten egg around edges of the wrap; gather up and pleat dumpling wrap around filling to form an open-topped pouch with the shrimp tail exposed.
4. Heat the wok on medium high heat for 20 seconds, and add 3 cups of oil into the wok. Lower shrimp purses into the wok one by one, and deep-fry them over medium high heat until they all turn golden brown. Place on a garnished plate.
5. Mix the dipping sauce ingredients together in a bowl. Serve shrimps purses with the dipping sauce.

Tips:
A few times practice may be necessary for beginners. Use some dumplings wraps to practice first.

Seafood Chrysanthemum Rolls

(4 servings)

Ingredients:

Peeled, de-veined shrimps	1 cup (large)
Imitation crabmeat	2 pieces
Spring roll wrappers	6 pieces
Tapioca flour	1 tbsp
Salt	¼ tsp
Beaten egg	1
Black sesame seeds	1 tbsp
Shredded lettuce	garnish

Seasoning:

Salt	¼ tsp
White pepper	⅛ tsp
Tapioca flour	1 tbsp
Sesame oil	¼ tsp

Method:

1. Rub shrimps with tapioca flour and salt for a few minutes, then rinse well with water and wipe dry with a clean towel.
2. Chop the imitation crab meat and crumble apart.
3. Flatten and mash shrimp with the flat of a cleaver, then mix with seasoning. Stir in one direction until the shrimp paste has a sticky consistency. Add the crumbled imitation crabmeat into the shrimp paste, and refrigerate for 1 hour.
4. Cut spring roll wrappers into 3 cm X 20 cm long strips with a pair of scissors. Roll and cut into 1.5 cm long alternately. Cut the 1.5 cm long edges in a curved manner so as to form flower pedals.
5. Brush the edges of each strip with beaten egg.
6. Knead 1 tbsp of shrimp paste into round shape ball. Surround with spring roll wrapper into three to four layers, like flower pedals.
7. Sprinkle some black sesame seeds on top.
8. Grease a baking pan, and place the chrysanthemum rolls onto pan. Spray some oil on top.
9. Preheat oven to 400°F, bake for 15 minutes until rolls turn golden brown.

Tips:

Only very dry shrimps can make a good shrimp paste. Too much water in the shrimp will make the shrimp paste difficult to stick together and not tender enough.

Steamed Mung Bean Threads with Garlic Prawns

(4 servings)

Ingredients:

Dried mung bean threads	2 bundles
Freshwater prawns	8 large
Minced garlic	4 cloves
Chicken stock	1 cup
Salt	¼ tsp
White pepper	⅛ tsp

Method:

1. Soak mung bean threads in cold water for 30 minutes. Drain in a strainer.
2. Mince garlic and set aside.
3. Wash and pat dry the prawns, trim off the legs and the tentacles of the prawns (still in shell); use a small shape knife to cut the back through the shell about ⅔ of the prawn depth; and de-vein the prawn simultaneously. Season prawns with salt and white pepper.
4. Bring chicken stock to a boil in a pot, then lower the mung bean threads into pot and boil for 1 minute. Use a pair of chopsticks or a pair of tongs to remove the mung bean threads, then arrange the mung bean threads on a serving plate. Reserve about 2 tbsp of chicken stock for later use.
5. Place the de-veined prawns on top of the mung bean threads and put 1 tsp of minced garlic on the middle of the prawns evenly. Pour ½ tsp of chicken stock on the minced garlic.
6. Boil 2 cups of water in a wok, put the steam rack inside the wok and steam the prawns for 5 minutes.
7. Serve hot.

Tips:

Do not boil mung bean threads too long in the chicken stock as it only takes a few minutes to cook.

The head of freshwater prawns are very big and juicy, thus it is preferred not to trim the head off. There is a very pointy and sharp needle-like hard shell close to the tail. Make sure to cut it off as well as all the tentacles for safety reasons.

Fried Soft Shell Crabs with Salty Egg Sauce

(4 servings)

Ingredients:

Frozen soft-shell crabs	4 whole
Chinese parsley	a few
Oil	3 cups

Seasoning:

Salt	¼ tsp
Chicken powder	¼ tsp
Sesame oil	¼ tsp
Sugar	½ tsp
White pepper	⅛ tsp
Ginger wine	1 tsp

Batter:

Beaten egg	1
Flour	1 cup
Water	1 cup
Salt, white pepper	a pinch of each

Sauce:

Cooked salty duck eggs	2
Chicken stock	1 cup
Sugar	½ tsp
Sesame oil	¼ tsp
Cornstarch	1 tsp

Method:

1. Thaw the crabs as package indicates. Remove the stomach flaps and clean them with a small brush. Discard the gills and inedible interior. Wipe dry with paper towel.
2. Season crabs with salt, chicken powder, sugar, sesame oil, white pepper, and ginger wine in a bowl for 20 minutes.
3. Meanwhile, mix beaten egg, water, flour, salt, and pepper together as batter mixture.
4. Discard the salty duck egg white, and only use the egg yolk. Use a blender to blend duck egg yolk, chicken stock, sugar, sesame oil, and cornstarch together.
5. Heat a wok on high heat for 30 seconds, and then add 3 cups of oil. Turn to medium high heat. Dip crabs in batter, then lightly dredge crabs in flour and shake gently to remove excess batter. Deep-fry about 3 minutes, until crabs turn light brown. Turn crabs often. Remove from oil and drain fried crabs on paper towels to remove excess oil. Arrange on a serving plate.
6. In a small sauce pan, bring the blended sauce mixture to a boil. Pour over fried crabs, and garnish with Chinese parsley.

Tips:

Most of the salty duck eggs sold in markets are pre-cooked. If you purchase any raw salty duck eggs, make sure to cook it thoroughly before serving. Salty egg is very salty, as its name indicates, so use it sparingly.

Steamed Crab with Minced Pork and Egg

(4 servings)

Ingredients:

Fresh crab	1 whole
Minced pork	8 oz
Beaten egg	2 (Extra large)
Cooked salty duck egg	1
Water	3 tbsp
Oil	1 tsp

Seasoning:

Salt	¼ tsp
Sugar	¼ tsp
Soy sauce	½ tsp
White pepper	⅛ tsp

Method:

1. Clean and cut the crab into 4 pieces, and save the top shell.
2. Discard the salty duck egg white, just use the egg yolk and cut the egg yolk into tiny pieces.
3. Season the minced pork with salt, sugar, soy sauce and white pepper. Add beaten egg, preserved duck egg yolk, and water into the minced pork and mix well.
4. Use 1 teaspoon of oil to brush a deep dish. Pour the minced pork mixture into the dish. Place crab shell on top of the minced pork in the middle.
5. Bring 3 cups of water to a boil in a wok, place a steam rack into the wok; and then steam the minced pork for 15 minutes. Serve hot.

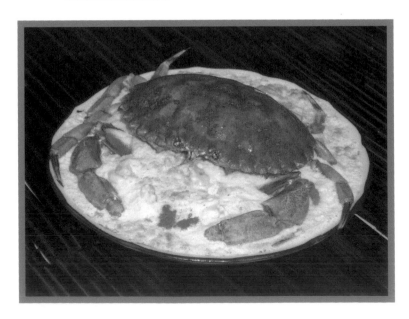

Tips:
It is highly suggested to use fresh crab because the fresh crab juice will be soaked into the minced pork.
Egg and water proportion should be 2:1.
Cooked salty duck egg is sold in Asian markets.

Scallop Wontons with Lime Butter Sauce

(4 servings)

Ingredients:

Jumbo scallops	8 pieces
Shanghai wonton wrappers	16 pieces
Sweet basil	4 stalks
Salt	pinch
White pepper	pinch
Egg white	1
Water	4 cups
Oil	1 tbsp

Sauce:

Chopped basil leaves	2 tbsp
Lime juice	2 - 3 tbsp
Lime zest	3 tbsp
Chicken stock	3 tbsp
Sugar	2 tsp
Butter	4 tbsp
White pepper	pinch

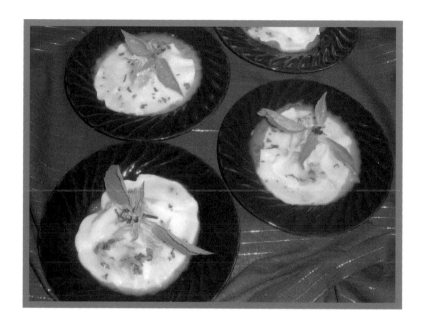

Method:

1. Wash and wipe dry the scallops and then season with salt and pepper.
2. Wash the basil and pick 8 pieces of the big leaves for later use; finely chop the 4-6 leaves. Save the top for decoration.
3. Use a grater to zest the lime and reserve; cut lime in half, and then squeeze the lime juice into a bowl.
4. Place one wonton wrapper on a plate, place 1 basil leaf on top, and then top with one scallop. Brush egg white on the edge and cover with one wonton wrapper on top. Make 8 scallop wonton dumplings.
5. Boil 4 cups of water with 1 tbsp of oil in a large pot, and then lower the scallop wontons into the pot after the water brings to boil. Boil for 5 minutes or until they are floating on top of the water surface. Remove from water and arrange on a small serving plates.
6. Heat a small pot on medium heat; bring to a boil lime juice, 1 tbsp of lime zest, chicken stock, sugar. Turn off the heat and add butter until it is melted, season with white pepper and sprinkle some finely chopped basil over it. Mix well and pour 1 tbsp of butter sauce on top of each scallop wonton dumplings.
7. Garnish with lime zest and basil leaves.

Tips:

Lower wontons into pot after the water has boiled. If the water is not boiling, the wontons will stick on the bottom of the pot easily. Adding oil to the water can prevent wontons sticking together.

Shanghai wonton wrappers are thicker than regular wonton wrappers. No matter how thick the wonton wrappers are, as long as they are floating on top of the water surface when they are being boiled, they are fully cooked.

Boiled Clams with Sake

(4 servings)

Ingredients:

Fresh Mahogany clams	1 ½ pounds
Japanese sake	¾ cup
Chicken stock	1 cup
Water	¼ cup
Minced garlic	2 tbsp
Chinese parsley	2 tbsp
Red chili	1 piece
Oil	1 tbsp

Method:
1. Clean clam shells with a small brush under tap water. Discard any bad clams. Drain them in a strainer.
2. Heat 1 tbsp of oil on high heat in a wok and sauté minced garlic and Chinese parsley for 30 seconds. Then add red chili, sake, water and chicken stock in to the wok, and bring to a boil.
3. Add clams into the wok, cover with lid, and cook for about 5-7 minutes, until the clam shells are all opened and done.
4. Ladle into a large bowl and serve hot.

Tips:
The clam soup is very delicious and can be served with rice. Other kinds of clams can be used instead of Mahogany clams. Choose the fresh and big size clams are recommended.

Stir-fried Tuna Fish and Celery with Hot Black Bean Sauce

(4 servings)

Ingredients:

Tuna fish fillet	12 oz
Celery	¼ piece
Minced garlic	2 cloves
Fermented black bean	2 tbsp
Shredded ginger	4 slices
Shredded red chilies	2 pieces
Hot bean paste	1 tsp
Shao Hsing wine	1 tbsp
Water	3 cups
Salt	¼ tsp
Sugar	¼ tsp
Oil	4 tbsp

Sauce:

Oyster sauce	1 tbsp
Salt	¼ tsp
Sugar	1 tsp
Cornstarch	2 tsp
Dark soy sauce	1 tbsp
White pepper	⅛ tsp
Sesame oil	a few drops
Water	½ cup

Method:

1. Wash celery and cut into 2 inches pieces. Cut tuna fish fillet into 2 inches long pieces as well. Mix the sauce in a bowl and set aside. Crush the fermented black bean with a fork.
2. Bring 3 cups of water to a boil in a pot with salt and sugar, and then blanch the celery for 2 minutes. Remove celery and discard the water.
3. Heat a wok on medium high heat for 30 seconds, add 4 tbsp of oil in a wok; and then add tuna fish to the wok, frying each side for 2 minutes, dish up the fish on a plate and set aside.
4. Leave 2 tbsp of oil in the wok, turn the heat to medium high, sauté minced garlic, fermented black bean, ginger, red chilies, and hot bean paste into the wok for a minute. Then add celery and fish into the wok, using Chinese spatula to toss well. Add Shao Hsing wine into it, and then put the prepared sauce in the wok and let it cook until the sauce is thickened.
5. Dish up on a serving plate.

Tips:

Do not keep flipping the fish while cooking; otherwise, the fish will become flaky .

Mussels with Black Bean Garlic Sauce

(4 servings)

Ingredients:

Half shell green mussels	12 pieces
Chicken stock	1 cup
Minced garlic	1 tsp
Fermented black bean	1 tbsp
Chopped red bell pepper	½ piece
Chopped green bell pepper	½ piece
Chopped spring onion	1 stalk
Oil	1-2 tbsp
Shao Hsing wine	1 tsp

Seasoning:

Salt	½ tsp
Ground black pepper	¼ tsp
Cornstarch	1 tbsp
Water	4 tbsp

Method:
1. Thaw mussels, rinse and pat dry. Mix all seasoning ingredients in a small bowl for later use.
2. Bring chicken stock to a boil in a pot, and then add mussels. Boil for 4 minutes, then drain mussels with a Chinese strainer and set aside.
3. Heat a wok over high heat for 30 seconds, add 1-2 tablespoon of oil into the wok, sauté garlic, black bean, and spring onion for a minute, and then add red and green bell pepper into the wok, sauté for another 2 minutes. Put mussels back into the wok; mix well with all the ingredients using Chinese spatula. Sprinkle wine over the mussels. Add seasonings and stir-fry everything in the wok until the sauce is thickened.
4. Dish up and serve hot.

Tips:
Do not overcook mussels; otherwise the mussels become very hard and tough to eat.

Pan-fried Potato Cakes with Chinese Sausage and Dried Shrimps

(4 servings)

Ingredients:

Potato	1 large
Dried shrimps	2 tbsp
Chinese chicken sausage	1 piece
Spring onion	1 stalk
Chicken powder	¼ tsp
Flaxseed	2 tbsp

Method:

1. Soak dried shrimps with warm water for 30 minutes, and mince after it becomes softened.
2. Boil 1 cup of water in a wok to blanch Chinese sausage for 2-3 minutes, and then mince it.
3. Chop the spring onion into tiny pieces.
4. Peel and wash the potato, cut into big pieces. Boil about 2 cups of water in a wok, put the steam rack inside the wok and cover with lid; steam the potato for 10 minutes. Mash it and mix with minced dried shrimp, Chinese sausage, spring onion, and chicken powder. Mix well.
5. Shape 1-2 tablespoonful of mixture into round shape with hands, and then sprinkle with some flaxseed on top.
6. Preheat oven to 450°F, grease a baking pan, place the potato cakes on the pan and bake them for 12-15 minutes, until golden brown.

Tips:

The baking method can be substituted by pan frying over medium high heat for 10-12 minutes.

Blanching Chinese sausages can remove the excess oil.

There are different kinds of Chinese sausages in the Asian market. Pork sausages can be used too.

Stir-fried Sugar Snap Peas with Lotus Root and Wolfberries

(4 servings)

Ingredients:

Sugar snap peas	½ pound
Lotus root	1 section
Wolfberries	2 tbsp
Oil	2 tbsp
Water	2 cups
Ginger	3 slices
Salt	1¼ tsp
Sugar	¼ tsp
Sesame oil	a few drops
Cold water with ice cubes	3 cups

Method:
1. Wash and peel off the hard ends of the sugar snap peas. Wash and peel the lotus root; and then trim the ends and cut it into thin strips.
2. Rinse the wolfberries and soak in tap water for 30 minutes.
3. Bring 2 cups of water with 1 tsp of salt in a wok to a boil. Add the sugar snap peas and boil for 5 minutes. Then remove the peas and soak in an ice cold water bath to stop them from continuing to cook. Drain the snap peas in a strainer.
4. Put 2 tbsp of oil in a wok on high heat, sauté ginger slices for about 10 seconds, add shredded lotus root and stir-fry for 2 minutes; and then add sugar snap peas and wolfberries into the wok and stir-fry for another minute. Keep stirring constantly with a Chinese spatula while cooking.
5. Combine salt, sugar, sand sesame oil with the vegetables and stir-fry for another minute. Dish up and serve hot.

Tips:
Sugar snap peas can be substituted by long green beans. Soak the sugar snap peas in cold water not only can stop them from continuing to cook, but also keeps the color brightly.

Lotus root has a lot of mud on the surface, wash it thoroughly with tap water is necessary.

Deep-fried Eggplants with XO Sauce

(4 servings)

Ingredients:

Japanese eggplant	1 piece
Oil	2 cups
XO sauce	1–2 tbsp

Batter:

All-purpose flour	⅔ cup
Tapioca flour	3 tbsp
Baking soda	1 tsp
Sugar	1 tsp
Salt	½ tsp
Five spice powder	¼ tsp
Water	1 cup
XO sauce	2tbsp

Method:

1. Prepare the batter; mix all-purpose flour, tapioca flour, baking soda, sugar, salt, five spice powder, water, and XO sauce together into a thin batter. Let the batter stand for 20 minutes.
2. Wash and cut eggplant into big slices.
3. Heat 2 cups of oil over high heat in a wok, dip the eggplant slices into the batter, lightly dip eggplant pieces in flour mixture and shake gently to remove excess batter. Lower eggplant into hot oil gently and one at a time. Deep-fry each piece for 5 minutes.
4. Remove eggplants and drain excess oil on paper towel. Place on serving plate.
5. Garnish XO sauce on top of each fried eggplant piece.

Tips:

Eggplants can turn into rusty in color very easily, so handle them quickly by slicing them and then dip into batter as soon as possible. Otherwise, the eggplant needs to soak in lightly salted water in order to prevent oxidization.

Baked Assorted Vegetables in Portuguese Sauce

(4 servings)

Ingredients:

Broccoli crown	1 small
Yellow squash	1 whole
Baby carrots	1 cup
Button mushrooms	1 cup
Water	3 cups
Salt	¼ tsp
Coconut milk	½ cup
Turmeric powder	1 tsp
Milk	½ cup
Butter	2 tbsp
All-purpose flour	2 tbsp

Seasoning:

Salt, white pepper, sugar and chicken powder   ½ tsp each

Method:

1. Wash and cut broccoli crown and yellow squash into pieces. Wipe clean the button mushrooms with a damp towel; then wash and pat dry the baby carrots.
2. Preheat oven to 425°F.
3. Boil 3 cups of water with ¼ tsp of salt in a wok over high heat, cover with lid, and then blanch broccoli crown, yellow squash, baby carrots, and button mushrooms for 2 minutes. Discard water and drain the vegetables very well. Arrange assorted vegetables in an oven safe bowl.
4. Heat a small pot over medium low heat, melt butter in the pot and stir fry flour until the flour becomes a thick paste without lumps.
5. Add coconut milk, turmeric powder, and milk to flour. Then add salt, white pepper, sugar, and chicken powder, and cook for 5 minutes. Keep stirring mixture constantly with a whisk.
6. Pour the sauce over the assorted vegetables. Bake at 425°F for 15-18 minutes until the surface turns golden brown.

Tips:

Do not blanch the assorted vegetables too long, since it will be cooked in the oven.

Steamed Eggs with Five Color Egg Tofu

(4 servings)

Ingredients:

Egg tofu	1 piece
Beaten egg	4 large
Chicken stock	⅓ cup
Diced carrots	½ piece
Sweet corn, green peas	¼ cup each
Diced red bell pepper	⅓ piece
Dried cloud ears	8 pieces
Ginger	3 slices
Shao Hsing wine	1 tsp
Water	4 cups
Salt, sugar	½ tsp each
Oil	1 tsp

Sauce:

Oyster flavored sauce, soy sauce	1 tbsp each
Sugar, cornstarch	1 tsp each
Water	3 tbsp

Method:

1. Soak cloud ears for 30 minutes in warm water. Once the cloud ears have puffed up to a larger size, remove the hard parts and cut into small pieces.
2. Boil 2 cups of water with ginger, Shao Hsing wine, salt, and sugar in a pot. Then boil carrots, sweet corn, green peas, cloud ears and diced red bell pepper for 3 minutes. Discard the water and drain all the vegetables with a strainer. Mix the sauce ingredients in a small bowl for later use.
3. Grease four small serving bowls. Cut egg tofu into 1 cm-thick slices and arrange them inside the serving bowls. Mix beaten egg and chicken stock together; pour egg mixture into the small serving bowls evenly. The eggs should be able to cover the tofu. Scoop out the small bubbles on top of the eggs.
4. Bring 2 cups of water to a boil in wok; place a steam rack in the wok with a plate on top and cover with a wok lid. Lower the serving bowls onto the plate over the steam rack when the water is boiling, cover with the wok lid, and steam for 8 minutes.
5. Meanwhile, heat 1 tsp of oil in a small pan, sauté all cooked vegetables in the pan for 1 minute, and then pour all of the sauce ingredients into the pan. Let it bring to a boil, until the sauce is thickened.
6. Remove the four serving bowls from the wok. Pour the sauce and vegetables on top of the steamed egg tofu. Serve hot.

Tips:

Ginger and wine can be used to alleviate the frozen and muddy smell of the assorted vegetables. Egg and chicken stock proportion should be 2:1. Too much chicken stock will prevent the egg from cooking firmly.

Deep-fried Tofu
with Spicy Salt

(4 servings)

Ingredients:

Firm tofu	1 box
Oil	3 cups
Spicy salt	1 tsp
Shredded spring onion	garnish

Batter:

All-purpose flour	½ cup
Tapioca flour	2 tbsp
Baking powder	½ tsp
Water	¼ cup
Five spice powder, salt	¼ tsp each
Spring onion	1 stalk
Red chili	1 piece

Spicy salt:
Heat a wok over medium high for 30 seconds; do not add any oil or water. Put 2 tbsp of salt and 1 tsp of five spice powder in a wok, stir constantly with a Chinese spatula for 1 minute. Dish up and reserve.

Method:
1. Wash and pat dry the red chili and spring onion, then finely chop them.
2. Mix all-purpose flour, tapioca flour, baking powder, water, five spice powder, and salt in a bowl. Let it stand for 20 minutes. Then add the chopped red chili and spring onion in the batter mixture.
3. Cut the firm tofu into 9 pieces. Dip into the batter.
4. Heat 3 cups of oil in a wok over high heat until the temperature reaches 425°F, and gently lower the tofu into the wok to deep-fry until golden brown and hard crust is formed. Remove fried tofu and drain on paper towel.
5. Transfer deep-fried tofu on a serving plate. Sprinkle some spicy salt on top of fried tofu and garnish with shredded spring onion. Serve hot.

Tips:
The crispy coating on the tofu tends to become soft in a short time, because of the hot steam enclosed and the wetness of tofu. Serve immediately for better taste.

Curry Tofu

Ingredients:

Hard tofu	1 box
Onion	½ piece
Green bell pepper	1 half
Red bell pepper	1 half
Carrot	1 half
Potato	1 whole
Curry powder	1 tbsp
All-purpose flour	1 tbsp
Ketchup	2 tbsp
Low-fat milk	1 cup
Dried bay leaf	1 piece
Unsalted butter	2 tbsp
Salt	1 tsp
Oil	2 cups

Seasoning:

Black pepper	¼ tsp
Sugar, chicken powder	½ tsp each
Salt	⅓ tsp

Method:

1. Sprinkle salt all over tofu, and refrigerate for 2 hours.
2. Dry and cut tofu into 2 cm cubes. Cut onion, green bell pepper, red bell pepper, carrot, and potato into cubes of similar size to tofu cubes.
3. Heat 2 cups of oil in a pot on medium high heat and deep-fry the tofu until golden brown, set aside.
4. Use the same oil to deep-fry potato until golden brown and set aside as well.
5. Heat butter in a pan, stir-fry onion, green bell pepper, red bell pepper, and carrot for 3-5 minutes in medium high heat. Then add curry powder, flour, milk, and ketchup and mix well. Add seasoning and cook until smooth.
6. Add fried tofu and potato into the curry sauce. Cook for a few minutes.
7. Serve in a bowl.

Tips:

Sprinkling salt onto tofu is not only for the purpose of seasoning, but also to remove excess water from the tofu.
Using medium high heat to stir-fry curry will prevent curry from burning.
It is very easy to get burn the bottom of the pot, so heat control is very important.

Pei Par Tofu

(4 servings)

Ingredients:

Diced soft tofu	½ pack
Peeled, de-veined shrimp	10 pieces
Chinese mushroom	1 piece
Dried shrimps	1 tbsp
Egg white	1
Chinese parsley	a few
Broccoli crown	1 piece
Oil	2 tbsp
Water	2 cups
Salt, sugar	¼ tsp each

Seasoning for shrimps:

Salt	⅛ tsp
Tapioca flour	½ tsp

Sauce:

Oyster flavored sauce	1 tbsp
Salt	¼ tsp
Sugar	1 tsp
Water	½ cup
Tapioca flour	1 tbsp

Method:
1. Soak Chinese mushroom and dried shrimps in tap water for 1 hour. Drain both in a strainer. Rub mushroom with 1 tsp of tapioca flour, and then rinse well. Mince mushroom and dried shrimps. Wash the broccoli and cut into small pieces.
2. Use the flat side of a Chinese cleaver to mash shrimps into shrimp paste, add salt and tapioca, and then stir in one direction for a few minutes. Add egg white, minced mushroom, dried shrimps, and tofu into mashed shrimp and mix well.
3. Grease 8 ceramic Chinese soup spoons. Fill the spoons with the tofu mixture and place Chinese parsley on top of each tofu mixture, steam over boiling water for 10 minutes.
4. Meanwhile, boil 2 cups of water with salt and sugar in a pot, and cook broccoli crown for a few minutes until fully cooked. Drain broccoli and arrange on a serving plate. Prepare the sauce ingredients in a bowl for later use.
5. After 10 minutes steaming, use a knife to scoop out the steamed tofu from the soup spoons.
6. Heat a small non-stick pan with 2 tbsp of oil and pan-fry steamed tofu until both sides turn golden brown. Arrange tofu on the plate with broccoli. Heat the sauce in a pan until it boils and becomes thickened. Pour on top of the tofu and broccoli and serve.

Tips:
Use a Chinese cleaver to mash shrimp and only stir in one direction. Do not mince shrimp with a knife- blade, otherwise it will lose its texture.
In order to keep tofu in shape, pan fry one side at a time, and then turn over to fry another side. Do not keep turning the tofu.

Stir-fried Assorted Mushrooms with Baby Corn and Macadamia Nuts

(4 servings)

Ingredients:

King oyster mushrooms	2 pieces
Oyster mushrooms	1 cup
Canned straw mushrooms	1 can
Baby corns	8 pieces
Carrot slices	12 pieces
Macadamia nuts	½ cup
Minced garlic	1 tbsp
Ginger wine	2 tbsp
Water	3 cups
Oil	1 cup

Seasoning:

Sugar	½ tsp
Chicken powder	½ tsp
Salt	¼ tsp
Water	6 tbsp
Shao Hsing wine	1 tsp

Method:

1. Wipe king oyster mushrooms and oyster mushrooms with a damp towel and drain the canned straw mushrooms. Cut the king oyster mushrooms into 1 inch pieces, and cut a cross on top of the straw mushrooms. Cut baby corns into half and shape carrots into flower shapes with a cookie cutter.
2. Heat 1 cup of oil in a pot over medium high heat for 30 seconds, add macadamias nuts into the pot and deep-fry until the nuts turn light brown.
3. Boil 3 cups of water in a wok, and then add ginger wine. Place all the mushrooms into the wok and boil for 3 minutes. Remove assorted mushrooms from wok and drain well. Discard the water.
4. Heat a wok over high heat with 1 tbsp of oil. Sauté minced garlic for 10 seconds. Add carrot flowers and stir-fry for 30 seconds. Place assorted mushrooms and baby corns in the wok, sprinkle Shao Hsing wine on top, season with water, sugar, chicken powder, and salt, and stir-fry for 2 minutes. Then mix macadamia nuts to serve.

Tips:

Deep-frying macadamia nuts to a light brown color is enough, as the nuts will keep cooking themselves even after being removed from oil. Their color will change into a golden brown later.

Ginger wine can remove the muddy smell from the mushrooms.

Shrimp Fried Rice
in Pineapple Boat

(4 servings)

Ingredients:

Pineapple	1 whole
Beaten eggs	2
Spring onion	1 stalk
Green peas	¼ cup
Large shrimps	20 pieces
Cooked rice	3 cups
Water	2 cups
Oil	3 tbsp

Seasoning:

Chicken powder	½ tsp
Soy sauce	1 tsp

Method:

1. Cut ⅓ of the pineapple off, scoop out the flesh from the remaining ⅔ of the pineapple to make a pineapple boat. Save 1 cup of flesh for later use.
2. Finely chop the spring onion. Boil 2 cups of water and blanch the green peas for 2 minutes. Drain green peas from the boiling water and discard water.
3. Add 1 tbsp of oil in a non-stick skillet, soft-scramble the eggs, then remove from skillet and cut coarsely with a knife and reserve.
4. Heat a wok on high with 2 tbsp of oil for 30 seconds, add the cooked rice and stir-fry for few minutes; then add the shrimps, stirring for 2 minutes. Add green peas and spring onion to the rice and stir with chicken powder and soy sauce and soft-scrambled egg.
5. Lastly, mix well with pineapple flesh thoroughly. Dish on a pineapple boat to serve.

Tips:
Do not put too much pineapple juice in the rice, otherwise the rice will become very soggy and the rice will stick to the bottom of the wok.

Vegetable Chicken Rice

(4 servings)

Ingredients:

Chicken meat	2 pieces
	(boneless and skinless)
Baby bok choy	2 cups
Dried Chinese mushrooms	6 pieces
Ham hock	1 piece
Water	2 cups
Tapioca flour	1 tbsp
Oil	2 tbsp

Rice:

Long grain rice	2 cups
Water	2 cups

Seasoning for chicken:

Salt	½ tsp
White pepper	⅛ tsp
Soy sauce	1 tsp
Sesame oil	½ tsp

Seasoning for Chinese mushrooms:

Salt	¼ tsp
Sugar	¼ tsp
Wine	⅛ tsp
Sesame oil	a few drops

Method:

1. Soak dried Chinese mushrooms in warm water for 30 minutes, then cut the hard stems off. Clean the Chinese mushrooms by rubbing 1 tbsp of tapioca flour on them and rinse well. Season with salt, sugar, wine, and sesame oil for 20 minutes.
2. Heat 2 cups of water in a wok, lower the steam rack inside the wok and cover with wok lid. Place the mushrooms inside the wok after the water boils. Steam for 20 minutes. Remove from wok, and dice mushrooms into 1 cm pieces after the mushrooms have cooled.
3. Clean and dice the chicken meat into 1 cm pieces, then season chicken with salt, white pepper, soy sauce, and sesame oil for 20 minutes.
4. Wash and shred baby bok choy into thin strips.
5. Trim the fat and skin of the ham hock away, leaving only the meat. Finely chop the ham hock meat.
6. Heat 2 tbsp of oil in a wok and sauté diced chicken meat, Chinese mushrooms, ham hock meat, and Baby bok choy for 4 minutes. Set aside for later use.
7. Cook 2 cups of rice with 2 cups of water in a rice cooker. Lower the sautéed meats and vegetables into rice cooker when the rice is 70% done.
8. Mix all the ingredients with the rice when the rice is done cooking.

Tips:

Less water is needed to cook the rice in this recipe, as the meats and vegetables will release more water into the rice during the cooking process.

Easy Yin Yang Fried Rice

(4 servings)

Ingredients:

Cooked rice	4 cups
Beaten eggs	3
Oil	3 tbsp
Green peas	8 pods

Yin's ingredients:

Large shrimp	16 pieces
Onion	1 half
Salt	¼ tsp
Cornstarch	1 tbsp
Oil	1 tbsp
Cream of chicken soup	1 can
Water	½ can

Yang's ingredients:

Chicken breast meat	2 pieces
Salt	pinch
White pepper	pinch
Oil	1 tbsp
Tomatoes	2 medium
Worcestershire sauce	1 tsp
Cream of tomato soup	1 can
Water	½ can

Method:

1. Peel and de-vein large shrimps. Rub salt and cornstarch on shrimps, rinse well, and then wipe dry with paper towel.
2. Shred the chicken breast meat into thin strips. Season shredded chicken meat with a pinch of salt and white pepper. Cut the onion and tomatoes into thin strips.
3. Heat a wok on high for 30 seconds. Add oil into the wok and heat for a few seconds. Stir-fry the cooked rice in the wok for about 8 minutes. Add the beaten eggs and stir well. Cook until the eggs are done. Dish on four deep round plates. Set aside.
4. Heat a non-stick pan over high with 1 tbsp of oil, and sauté onion until it is softened. Then add shrimps into pan and sauté for 2 minutes. Pour can of cream of chicken soup and water into the pan; stir well until it boils. Serve over one half side of the rice.
5. Heat a non-stick pan over high with 1 tbsp of oil and sauté chicken for 5 minutes. Then add tomatoes and sauté for 2 minutes. Add a can of tomato soup, Worcestershire sauce, and water into the pan; stir well until it boils and cook for another 2 minutes. Serve over the other half side of the rice.
6. In a bowl, add a cup of water and the green pea pods in it, and then microwave for 40 seconds. Garnish green pea pods on top of the rice to form a Yin Yang symbol.

Tips:
Use aluminum foil to form an "S" shape and place it on top of the middle of the rice as a divider. Therefore, when pouring the sauce over the rice, you can avoid having the sauce mix up. Also, a large deep round plate can be used instead of 4 small round plates

Fried Rice with Assorted Meats and Vegetables in Gravy

(4 servings)

Ingredients:

Diced chicken	1 piece
Peeled, de-veined shrimps	8 pieces
Roasted duck meat	4 tbsp
Chinese mushrooms	2 pieces
Dried scallops	2 pieces
Green peas	4 tbsp
Beaten eggs	2
Cooked rice	4 cups
Salt	¼ tsp
Cornstarch	1 ¼ tbsp
Oil	3 tbsp

Seasoning for mushrooms:

Salt, sugar, sesame oil, wine	1/8 tsp each

Seasoning for chicken:

Salt, sugar, cornstarch	¼ tsp each
White pepper, sesame oil	a pinch of each

Seasoning for shrimps:

Salt and corn starch	¼ tsp
White pepper and sesame oil	pinch

Sauce:

Chicken stock	1 cup
Dark soy sauce, cornstarch1	tbsp each
Sugar	1 tsp

Method:

1. Dice chicken and season chicken with salt, sugar, cornstarch, white pepper and sesame oil for 20 minutes.
2. Rub shrimps with ¼ tsp of salt and ¼ tbsp of cornstarch, then rinse well and pat dry. Season with salt, cornstarch, white pepper and sesame oil for 20 minutes.
3. Soak dried Chinese mushrooms for 30 minutes in warm water, rub 1 tbsp of cornstarch to clean mushrooms, and then cut off the hard stems. Season with salt, sugar, sesame oil, and wine for 20 minutes.
4. Soak dried scallops for 30 minutes in water, and then break into tiny pieces.
5. Heat 2 cups of water in a wok; place the steam rack inside wok, then steam Chinese mushrooms and dried scallops together for 30 minutes. Dice Chinese mushrooms after it had cooled down.
6. Diced the roasted duck meat.
7. Boil 1 cup of water, and blanch green peas for 2 minutes. Discard water and reserve for later use.
8. Prepare the sauce ingredients in a bowl.
9. Heat a wok on medium high for 20 seconds, add 2 tbsp of oil, and then stir-fry the cooked rice for 5 minutes. Add beaten eggs into the center of the wok, and stir-fry with rice until eggs are done and dry. Place the fried rice in a deep dish.
10. Heat a wok with 1 tbsp of oil over medium high and stir-fry chicken for 3 minutes. Then add shrimps, steamed dried scallops, diced roasted duck, and diced mushrooms into the wok and stir-fry until they are done. Pour the green peas and sauce back into the wok. Brings to a boil, and cook until the sauce is thickened a bit.
11. Pour over the fried rice.

Tips:

Green peas can be substituted by Chinese kale stems or any other vegetables. Roasted duck meat can be substituted by Chinese BBQ pork. Use the ingredients which are most readily available to you.

Chicken and Mushrooms Oats Congee

(4 servings)

Ingredients:

Rice	½ cup
Quick oats	½ cup
Water	12 cups
Chicken breast meat	2 pieces
Chinese mushrooms	12 pieces
Chinese parsley	garnish
Shredded ginger	for garnish
Salt, white pepper	to taste
Cornstarch	2 tbsp

Seasoning for chicken:

Salt, soy sauce, sugar	½ tsp each
Sesame oil, ginger juice	½ tsp each

Seasoning for mushrooms:

Salt, sugar, soy sauce	½ tsp each
Sesame oil, Shao Hsing wine	¼ tsp each

Method:
1. Rinse rice and add with 12 cups of water into a big pot. Bring to a boil and then simmer for 1 hour.
2. Meanwhile, soak Chinese mushrooms in water for 30 minutes; then trim off the hard stems when they are softened. Rub 2 tbsp of cornstarch on the mushrooms, and then rinse well with water. Season mushrooms with wine, salt, sugar, and sesame oil, and then steam over boiling water on high heat for 20 minutes. Reserve.
3. Cut chicken into 1 inch cubes. Season chicken with seasonings for 30 minutes.
4. After simmering the congee for 1 hour, stir in quick oats, steamed mushrooms, and chicken into the congee and simmer for another 15 - 20 minutes.
5. Season to taste and garnish with shredded ginger and Chinese parsley.

Tips:
Do not stir the congee while simmering otherwise the congee will become very watery.
Rubbing Chinese mushrooms with cornstarch can remove the dirt that is trapped inside. Cornstarch can also be substituted by tapioca flour.

Crab Congee

(4 servings)

Ingredients:

Crabs	2 pieces
Rice	1 cup
Water	12 cups
Ginger	4 slices
Salt	⅛ tsp
White pepper	⅛ tsp

Seasoning:

Salt	¼ tsp (to taste)
White pepper	¼ tsp (to taste)

Method:

1. Put crabs into water and let them spill out dirt.
2. Wash and rinse rice, then add with 12 cups of water in a big pot. Use high heat to bring to a boil, and boil for 15 minutes without covering pot lid. Then turn the heat to medium and cover with lid, but leave a 1 inch gap between the pot and the lid to let steam out. Cook for 1 hour to 1 hour and 15 minutes, until the rice becomes mushy. Do not stir the congee.
3. Remove the stomach flaps and clean them with a small brush. Separate the top shell from the bottom and discard the gills and inedible interior. Cut the body in a half so that there are 2 pieces of each crab, each have legs attached. Slightly crush the big claws with the flat of a cleaver blade.
4. After congee has cooked for an hour, lower the crabs and ginger slices into the congee, and cook for another 15 minutes until the crabs are done.
5. Season with salt and white pepper to taste.
6. Serve hot.

Tips:

To clean crabs thoroughly, soak in water while cleaning to allow all the dirt to dissolve. Make sure that the crabs are very clean before putting them into the congee. Do not stir or add any thing into the congee while it is still cooking, otherwise the congee will stick to the bottom of the pot.

Flat Rice Noodles with Pork in Gravy

(4 servings)

Ingredients:

Fresh rice noodles	1 pound
Chinese kale	10 pieces
Sliced pork	6 oz
Salt	½ tsp
Sugar	½ tsp
Oil	3 tbsp
Water	3 cups

Marinade:

Salt	½ tsp
White pepper	⅛ tsp
Soy sauce	1 tsp
Tapioca starch	½ tsp
Water	3 tbsp

Gravy sauce:

Water	2 ½ cups
Sugar	2 tbsp
Dark soy sauce	2 tbsp
Soy sauce	2 tbsp
Oyster flavored sauce	1 tsp
Tapioca flour	4 tbsp
Sesame oil	1 tsp

Method:
1. Marinate sliced pork with all the marinade ingredients for 30 minutes. Wash and trim Chinese kale into 4 – 5 inches long.
2. Mix all the sauce ingredients in another bowl and wait for later use.
3. Boil 3 cups of water with salt and sugar in a pot, and blanch Chinese kale for a few minutes. Then rinse Chinese kale with cold tap water. Drain and set aside.
4. Heat a deep non-stick skillet over high hear for 20 seconds, add 3 tbsp of oil to the skillet, and then heat for another 30 seconds. Sauté pork for about 5-6 minutes. Add the Chinese kale and sauté for another 2 minutes. Add the sauce and fresh noodles to the skillet immediately, mix all the ingredients well and let cook for a few minutes, until the sauce is thickened like gravy.
5. Serve on a deep dish.

Tips:
Flat rice noodles can be very sticky to handle, so using a non-stick skillet allows you to minimize the oil used to cook this dish.
Fresh flat rice noodles are sold at large Asian Markets or Chinese noodle-making shops.
Add 1 more tablespoon of oyster flavored sauce if a saltier taste is desired.

Stir-fried Flat Rice Noodles with Sliced Beef

(4 servings)

Ingredients:

Sliced beef	4 oz
Fresh flat rice noodles	4 bowls
Bean sprouts	1 cup
Chinese chives	small bunch
Onion	1 small
Spring onion	1 stalk
Oil	5 tbsp

Seasoning for beef:

Baking soda	⅛ tsp
Soy sauce	1 tsp
Sugar	¼ tsp
Water	2 tbsp
Oil	1 tbsp
Cornstarch	1 tsp

Seasoning for noodles:

Dark soy sauce	2 tbsp
Soy sauce	1 tsp
Chicken powder	1 tsp

Method:

1. Season beef with baking soda, soy sauce, sugar, oil, water, and cornstarch for 30 minutes.
2. Wash all the vegetables. Trim away the heads and ends of the bean sprouts. Cut chives and spring onion into 3 inches long pieces. Shred onion into thin strips.
3. Heat 2 tbsp of oil on high in a wok, stir-fry onion for 3 minutes, add chives and stir-fry for 1 minute and then add bean sprouts to stir-fry with other vegetables for 30 seconds. Remove vegetables from the wok. Leave the oil in the wok and stir-fry beef until it is medium well. Take out for later use.
4. Heat 3 tbsp of oil on high in wok, add the flat rice noodles, and stir until no longer sticking together constantly. Add dark soy sauce, soy sauce, and chicken powder into wok, and mix well until noodles are colored evenly. Then add the beef and vegetables to the wok and mix well with the noodles.
5. Dish up and serve hot.

Tips:

Chives can be substituted by yellow chives.

The use of high heat is required in order to stir-fry everything quickly and thoroughly.

Fresh flat rice noodles are sold at large Asian Markets or Chinese noodle-making shops.

Fried Rice Noodles in Singapore Style

(4 servings)

Ingredients:

Rice stick noodles	1 pack
Shredded chicken	1 piece
Shredded Chinese BBQ pork	3 oz
Peeled, de-veined shrimps	12 pieces
Ginger	4 slices
Shredded onion	1 small
Shredded carrot	1 piece
Bean sprouts	1 cup
Chinese chives	small bunch
Curry powder	1 tsp
Chicken stock	⅔ cup
Light soy sauce	2 tsp
Dark soy sauce	2 tsp
Sugar	1 tsp
Sesame oil	1 tsp
Oil	3 tbsp

Method:

1. Use cold water to wash the rice noodles and allows it to become softened. Set aside.
2. Preheat a wok over high heat, add 2 tbsp of oil in a wok and sauté ginger for 20 seconds. Remove ginger and discard. Add chicken into the wok, sauté for 2-3 minutes, and then add onion, carrot, bean sprouts, and chives to stir-fry about 3 minutes, until they are done. Add shrimps and Chinese BBQ pork in, and stir-fry until the shrimps change color. Transfer the meat and vegetables into a plate for later use.
3. Heat a wok on medium high heat and add 1 tbsp of oil. Add curry powder, chicken stock, and the rice noodles into the wok, cook for 5 minutes, and mix well with a pair of tongs, tossing constantly. Add light soy sauce, dark soy sauce, sugar, and sesame oil mix well with the rice noodles, and cook for 1–2 minutes. Then add all the cooked meat and vegetables into the noodle and toss well.
4. Dish up and serve hot.

Tips:

Rice noodles can become soggy very easily. However, since this is a dry stir-fry noodle, it should neither be juicy nor soggy.

Chinese BBQ pork (Char Siu) is sold at Chinese rotisserie shops and restaurants. Cooked ham can be used to substitute Chinese BBQ pork.

Essential Ingredients in Hong Kong Home Cooking

Baby Bok Choy: Also called siu bok choy in Cantonese, the name refers to its size. A lighter green version of baby bok choy, known as Shanghai bok choy, has more of a bitter taste and tenderness than Bok Choy.

Bok Choy: A type of cabbage, which has white stem and dark green leaf, available in most supermarkets. Besides being used in soups and stir-fries, you'll also find it in braised dishes.

Bean Sprouts: In Cantonese it is called "Nga Choi", which are the youngest sprouts of the mung beans. Bean spouts are widely used in Chinese cooking. When using bean sprouts, try not to cook then longer than 30 second, for they will lose their crunchiness. To avoid its musty-smell, blanch it in hot boiling water for 30 seconds and then soak it in cold ice water, and just add on a cooked dish and toss well before dish up.

Mung Bean Threads: It is made from the mung bean starch, and often used for hot pot and salads.

Chinese Broccoli: It is one of the most commonly used vegetables in the Chinese kitchen. It looks like Choy Sum, but it has deeper green colored leaves. It is very tough, so it should be blanched before cooking.

Chinese Mushrooms: Chinese black mushrooms can range in colors from light brown, dark brown, to grayish. They are frequently speckled. Chinese black mushrooms also range in price from moderate to quite expensive. Before use, soak them in warm water for thirty minutes or longer and then remove the stems. Since the mushrooms have a lot of dirt trapped inside, Chinese chefs use tapioca flour or cornstarch to rub gently over the soaked mushroom and then rinse well. It is necessary to pre-cook mushrooms if it is intended for stir-fried dishes. Season the mushrooms with salt, sugar, soy sauce, and ginger wine and steam for 30 minutes before stir-frying with other vegetables.

Chinese Parsley: Chinese parsley, or cilantro, are the leaves of the coriander plant. Chinese cooks use cilantro in soups, stir-fries, and frequently as a garnish. It has a very strong flavor.

Chinese Sausages: Chinese sausages, or in Cantonese called "Lap Cheong", are usually made from pork, chicken, or duck liver meat. They are smaller than western sausages and have a sweet-salty flavor.

ChinKiang Vinegar: It is made from glutinous rice and has a sharp spicy flavor, similar to Worcestershire sauce with Balsamic vinegar. It also called "Zhenjiang" vinegar.

Dried Cloud Ears: These are brown-black fungi, which are usually sold in dried form. Soak them in warm water for at least 15 minutes and they will puff up into a larger size. It is best cooked in soups and stir-fries.

Choy Sum: Similar to bok choy, choy sum is recognizable by its small yellow flowers and medium size green leaves. Also known as Chinese flowering cabbage, it has a sweet, mustard flavor. While the stems of Choy Sum are generally preferred, you can eat the leaves as well, but not the flowers. Choy sum can be used in braised and stir fried dishes.

Cornstarch: It is a fine white powder is made from corn kernels. It is used in marinades, thickening, and frying. The amount of cornstarch is determined by the thickness of the sauce.

Curry Powder: A powder made by grinding and blending various herbs and spices, including cardamom, cinnamon, cumin, cloves, fenugreek, red peppers, nutmeg, and mace.

Dried Galangal Powder: It is a small tender root, quite like ginger but has a very fresh smell, like coriander. It comes in fresh ginger root form or dried powder, which can be kept in an air tight jar for a long time. It is very common in South East Asian kitchens.

Dried Shrimps: These small sun-dried shrimps are used to lend its aromatic flavor to dishes. Wash and soak in hot water before use for 15-30 minutes depending on its size.

Fermented Bean Curd: It is made of salt, bean curd, red rice, and wine, and thus red in color. It is not spicy and is used for braising, deep frying and Chinese barbeque recipes.

Fermented Black Bean: It is strongly flavored and preserved in salt and spices, and is an important ingredient in Chinese cooking, especially Cantonese and Sichuan. They are soft with a salty and bitter flavor. It can be used to season, steamed, braised, and stir-fry. Salted black beans are sold in plastic bags or in cans in Asian markets. Soak in tap water for 15 minutes before use to reduce the salty taste. Chop or mash them for best results. It is always cooked with garlic to bring out a stronger flavor.

Five Spice Powder: It is a blend of spices, consisting of ground star anise, cloves, cinnamon, fennel seeds and Sichuan peppercorns. It is widely used in marinades, seasoning, and cooking. Cook five spice powder and salt over a dry-roasting wok to make spicy salt.

Fish Sauce: Fish sauce is a thin and salty liquid, which is made from salted fish. It is used in place of salt as a seasoning and dipping in many Asian recipes. Although primarily associated with Vietnamese and Thai cuisine, it is also used in parts of southern China and occasionally in Cantonese cooking.

Ginger: The roots of the ginger plants are probably one of the most used ingredients in Chinese kitchens. It has sharp and spicy flavor, which is used in soups, stir-fries, marinades, and even for garnishing. It is good with seafood as it can reduce the fishy odors. When purchasing ginger, look for a firm, smooth body without new buds, and without any darkening or wrinkled skin.

Ginger Wine: Peel the ginger roots' skin and pat dry. Blend ginger and Shao Hsing wine together in a blender, drain the juice by using a small strainer and store it in a jar. Ginger wine can be stored in the refrigerator for up to a month. Ginger wine is not only useful; for covering up strong seafood odors, but also can add the wine's flavor on the seafood.

Hoi Sin Sauce: It is made from soybean paste and flavored with garlic, sugar, chilies, as well as other spices and ingredients. Hoi sin sauce is used in cooking, glazing, and dipping. It is a key ingredient in many Chinese barbecue sauce recipes.

Leek: Leeks are milder and sweeter than onions. Usually, only the root end, or the white part is used in recipes, since it is the best part of this vegetable. The white adds a subtle touch to various dishes without masking other flavors. In order to accentuate the flavor from the leek, Hong Kong chefs prefer to dry it out by placing it on the counter for a few days, until the white part turns a bit yellow.

Lychee: It has been cultivated in China for thousands of years. This small fruit has deep red and brown colors with rough skin. The translucent jelly-like flesh surrounds a single inedible seed. There are different types of lychees sold in the market, since different Chinese provinces grow lychee. Fresh lychee is available during the summertime in Asian markets. However, if it's not available fresh, you can always substitute it in recipes with canned lychees, which are more widely accessible.

Oyster Flavored Sauce: A rich sauce made from boiled oysters and seasonings. This sauce has a savory flavor, which is used in meat and vegetable dishes and is an important ingredient in Hong Kong cooking. But nowadays, most of the oyster sauces are made with artificial flavor, so called oyster flavored sauce.

Preserved Duck Egg: These eggs are thicker-tasting than chicken eggs. It can be bought raw or cooked. In the US, most brands are already cooked and imported from China or Taiwan. It should always be completely cooked before being served. Chinese people usually eat salted duck eggs as an accompaniment to plain congee, but sometimes it can be used in other cooking methods, such as steaming or stir-frying with seafood.

Rock Sugar: It is crystallized raw sugar and has a light, yellowish color. Its flavor is lighter than refined sugar and is used in desserts and braised dishes. It is available in Asian groceries.

Rice Noodles: Made from ground rice and water, they are available fresh or dried. Thin dry rice stick noodles are called rice vermicelli. The think ones are called flat rice noodles, which comes in fresh or dry form as well. In Cantonese, the flat rice noodles are called "Ho Fan" or "Gao Teal". It can be cooked in soups, stir fried, or deep fried.

Sesame Oil: This aromatic amber-colored oil, made from pressed and toasted sesame seeds, is a popular ingredient in Asian cooking. Sesame oil is not ideal for use as cooking oil solely, since the flavor is too intense and burns quite easily. It is usually used as a seasoning and flavoring agent in the final stages of cooking.

Shallots: It is more aromatic and subtle in flavor than the onion, but does not have a strong flavor like garlic. It is as big as a garlic bulb, but the shallot only has two or three cloves in one piece. Shallots can be kept for up to 1 month when stored in a cool, dark, and dry place with good air circulation.

Shao Hsing Wine: It is rice wine, also known as Chinese cooking wine. Rice wines are usually lower in alcohol and popular in Chinese stir-fries and steamed dishes. It can bring up the flavor and fragrance of dishes and also reduce seafood odors.

Soy Sauce (Light and Dark): Soy sauce is made from fermented soy beans, wheat flour, water, and salt. The two main types of soy sauce are light and dark. As the name implies, light soy sauce is lighter in color. In Hong Kong Chinese cooking, it is used more often than dark soy sauce. Always use light soy sauce, so-called soy sauce in a recipe unless dark is specifically called for. Aged for a longer period of time, dark soy sauce is thicker and darker in color. It is also less salty than light soy. It is used in certain recipes to add color.

Spring Onion: Also known as scallions or green onions. Spring onions have been cultivated in China for over 2,000 years. It is an immature onion with long green stems and a small under-developed white bulb at the root end, both of which are edible. Because of its crisp, sharp fresh taste and its bright green and white color, it is used very often in Chinese cooking.

Tapioca Flour: Made from the starch of the cassava root. Tapioca flour is often used to make dumpling dough or as a thickening agent. In Hong Kong Chinese cooking, it is also used as a deep-fry flour, like all-purpose flour. Tapioca flour can also be substituted by cornstarch for thickening.

Tofu: Also called bean curd. Tofu is made from soy beans, which is extremely high in protein. Although quite bland in taste by itself, it absorbs the flavors of the food it is cooked with and is used in many dishes, from soups and sauces to stir-fries. Tofu comes in extra firm, firm, regular, soft, and extra soft form, which are suitable for different kinds of cooking.

Water Chestnuts: It is not a nut, but a crunchy and juicy vegetable with brown skin. Drain and rinse canned water chestnuts before using. You may also want to rinse them briefly in boiling water to get rid of the "tinny" taste from the can. They can be eaten raw or added to stir-fries. Sometimes, you may find them fresh in Asian markets, in which case you simply have to wash and peel the skins off.

About the Author

Mei-yin May Lewis was born in Hong Kong, the Chinese city that is a food paradise. She has always loved to cook for her friends and family, even before she had any formal training in cooking. She became a Certificate Mistress from the Northcote College of Education, Hong Kong, in 1992. In 1995, she obtained the degree of Bachelor of Education with Honors at the University of Liverpool, United Kingdom. In 1998, she obtained her Master Degree of Arts (Education) at the University of Hull, United Kingdom. In addition, she studied dim sum, baking and chef cooking at the Hong Kong and Kowloon Restaurant Union while living in Hong Kong. She has organized and taught Chinese cooking classes in Japan since 2003. She currently resides in California with her loving husband and son. She also has a cooking website http:// maymaycooking.tripod.com for her fans and students to communicate with.

LaVergne, TN USA
08 January 2010
169366LV00004B

9 781432 719715